NATIONAL BUS COMPANY DUAL PURPOSE VEHICLES

MICHAEL HITCHEN

AMBERLEY

First published 2019

Amberley Publishing
The Hill, Stroud
Gloucestershire, GL5 4EP

www.amberley-books.com

Copyright © Michael Hitchen, 2019

The right of Michael Hitchen to be identified as the Author of this work has been asserted in accordance with the Copyrights, Designs and Patents Act 1988.

ISBN 978 1 4456 8637 0 (print)
ISBN 978 1 4456 8638 7 (ebook)

All rights reserved. No part of this book may be reprinted or reproduced or utilised in any form or by any electronic, mechanical or other means, now known or hereafter invented, including photocopying and recording, or in any information storage or retrieval system, without the permission in writing from the Publishers.

British Library Cataloguing in Publication Data.
A catalogue record for this book is available from the British Library.

Typesetting by Aura Technology and Software Services, India. Printed in the UK.

Introduction

In the 1970s, the country was a much bigger place – at least as a far as the transport enthusiast was concerned. Distant national bus companies could be a mystery; indeed, in a time before the internet obtaining detailed information was a difficult pastime, so a young enthusiast was often confined to one's local company. A. M. Witton's well-known fleetbooks were often the starting point, being affordable and with lots of detail, though space for extra photographs was obviously limited. Reading these fleet lists gave a tantalising insight into operators that were totally different to the company I was familiar with. It was the publication of Ray Stenning's *National Bus Company Album* in 1979 that, to me, showed the enormous variety that existed in the company at the time. The first book devoted to the subject, and with more than a consideration for graphic design, it combined numerous photographs with intelligent captions, opening a door to the wider National Bus Company. There was an element of romance in the text, of long journeys to far-off towns, and it was this that sparked my interest in the NBC local coach.

Though many of the nation's bus companies were already in state ownerships, the 1966 Labour government published a white paper proposing the merger of the state's Transport Holding Company (THC) and privately owned British Electric Traction (BET) organisations into a single National Bus Company. Moreover, recommendations of this white paper formed part of the Transport Act 1968. As a result, the National Bus Company was formed for operations in England and Wales in 1969. At the same time, Scottish state bus operation were reorganised into the Scottish Bus Group.

In 1972, Fred Wood, the new chairman of the National Bus Company, had returned from North America with a lasting impression of the Greyhound Network and its pan-continent corporate image. The time had come for a modern corporate image. As a result, simplifications to either leaf green or poppy red were to be new base colours, though a number of companies – Midland General, Sunderland District, East Yorkshire and Jones of Aberbeeg, for instance, which used blue – were allowed to continue in their varying shades mostly for the short term, except for Jones, which retained it until the 1981 formation of National Welsh. After a short period wherein local interpretations could be found, the standard liveries were established: red or green with a 3-inch central white stripe for local buses; red/white or green/white for 'local coaches'; and all-over white for 'national' coaches, although the idea of yellow for these vehicles was considered. 'Local coach' was the NBC term for the so-called dual-purpose vehicle (occasionally also called a semi-coach) – a vehicle with coach-style seating in either a bus or coach body, used for stage operations. This was the reason these vehicles were so attractive, as they crossed between bus and coach in livery and type. The National Bus Company dual-purpose vehicles were as diverse as the constituent companies they belonged to. The vehicles were more attractive than the monotone types that served local services and the long-distance national network. Many older types soldiered on into the corporate era, sometimes looking a little incongruous in their modernised identity.

The introduction of New Bus Grant by the then Labour government led to the development of coach designs that complied with the bus grant compliant specification. Examples on lightweight chassis became popular with some independent operators. If they had a mix of bus and coach work, for instance, then these hybrids were ideal. However, most NBC companies opted for a traditional chassis and body combination fitted with obligatory two-fold doors and a destination box. To secure the grant (initially 25 per cent and later 50 per cent of first cost), the vehicles had to do at least 50 per cent of their mileage on stage carriage services for their first five years. This 'grant specification' meant future dual-purpose deliveries would almost always be coach-bodied vehicles, meaning the higher specification bus-bodied version was no longer an attractive alternative.

The National Bus Company was at the time the largest bus company in the world, so compiling any selection will always be difficult, but I have attempted through the various companies to show the variety that existed in the relatively short period between 1972 and 1986, when the corporate livery reigned across England and Wales. After a short period of local interpretation, 'local coach' livery instructions were straightforward – upper half white, lower half the adopted colour of the constituent fleet. In the early 1980s these rules were relaxed and new liveries were introduced, ranging from the venetian blind livery used by many companies to individual operator liveries, such as Crosville's two-tone green 'Town Lynx' interpretation of the dual-purpose livery. Around the mid-1980s, the NBC head office further relaxed liveries and in the period just prior to the 1986 privatisation came an explosion of schemes, including Wilts & Dorset's yellow and red, South Wales's dark red with gold serif fleet names, Midland Red's yellow 'Midland Express' and many more.

A mention of the companies that formed the NBC would not go amiss. Many long-established companies enjoyed a real sense of belonging in the areas they served, the majority with local identity names such as Trent, Ribble, Lincolnshire or Bristol, though the term Crosville may have seemed a little confusing unless you were from the North West or North and Mid Wales! Sadly these names would all disappear in a few short years.

Today we reflect on a valuable national asset that was sadly lost to dogma, resulting for many in a much reduced service. Certain political powers have moved to discredit nationalised industries, generally falsely, so let's hope that one day more enlightened minds bring back a state-serving joined-up transport system to serve the entire population. For readers that remember the National Bus Company, I hope this brings back some memories. For those not fortunate enough to, I hope it gives an insight into an interesting and varied organisation that once served most of England and Wales.

I hope you enjoy this selection from a bygone age, when our bus company offered a service not only to a larger travelling public, but to rural locations and the wider community, with a skilled workforce and a joined-up industry.

Thanks go to Dave Mant, Andrew Tucker, Michael Penn and Jeremy Chapter for helping with many difficult to find loose ends and to Alan Snatt, Grahame Wareham and Lindsay Young. Without their kind assistance, I could not have attempted this book. Thanks also go to the Transport Library/Omnibus Society for the use of a number of photographs.

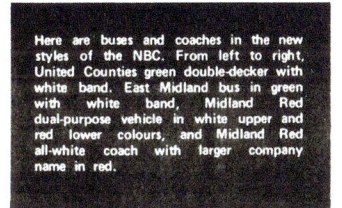

New semi-coach livery to be introduced soon

Here are buses and coaches in the new styles of the NBC. From left to right, United Counties green double-decker with white band, East Midland bus in green with white band, Midland Red dual-purpose vehicle in white upper and red lower colours, and Midland Red all-white coach with larger company name in red.

A new livery for dual-purpose single-deck vehicles owned by National Bus Company subsidiaries has been selected. This livery will be white above the waist and the company's colour below the waist. The company fleetname and National reflected "N" symbol will be displayed in the company's colour on the cove panels near the front of the vehicle. This is the same position as is used on single-deck service buses. Where the body design precludes this, the name will be displayed in white below the first side windows.

The NBC General Managers Conference of 1972 took place in October at the Post House, Leicester. Variations of the corporate livery, including for the first time the semi-coach livery applied to Midland Red Leyland Leopard 6412, were displayed to senior staff and approved. Interestingly, in the same month Midland Red painted a similar Leyland Leopard (6418) in these colours but reversed with white lower and red upper, although this was soon repainted in the new approved livery. Midland Red also enjoyed the distinction of the first NBC Central Activities 'white' coach, 5652 a CM6T – the famous home-built Motorway Express type. (Extract from December 1972 edition of *Bus*, NBC's in house newspaper)

Alder Valley 329 (428 DHO), Basingstoke Bus Station, 20 September 1974

Alder Valley was a creation of the NBC, formed in January 1972 when the National Bus Company combined the already state-owned Thames Valley Traction with the Aldershot & District Traction Company, a BET company. The full name was actually the Thames Valley & Aldershot Omnibus Company, but vehicles always carried Alder Valley as the fleet name. Originally part of the Aldershot & District fleet, 329 was a 1962 AEC Reliance fitted with Park Royal DP41F bodywork. Aldershot & District purchased a batch of fifteen AEC Reliance vehicles for their Farnham–London Victoria express coach service. Originally painted in a green and cream livery, they were soon displaced by 36-foot-long vehicles. In 1968 two vehicles were loaned to City of Oxford to ease their vehicle problems and in 1969–70 ten of the batch were sold to them. 329 was retained by A&D, becoming part of the merged Alder Valley fleet in 1972. (Alan Snatt)

Alder Valley 338 (474 FCG), Aldershot Garage, 25 May 1974

Arguably one of the most stylish vehicles in the NBC fleet, 338 was an AEC Reliance 4MU3RA with Park Royal C49F bodywork from a batch of fifteen such vehicles delivered to Aldershot & District in 1963. In 1966 came a further batch of five forty-nine-seat Reliance coaches of very similar appearance, though this time the bodies were built by Weymann. Delivered in A&D green/cream livery, many would feel this livery was not as attractive. These vehicles were unique within the NBC to Alder Valley, though East Kent and United Counties had similar looking types. 338 (474 FCG) was sold to Chiltern Queens, Woodcote, in 1975, who re-seated it to B53F and fitted twin headlights to the front. (Dave Mant)

Alder Valley 44 (FHO 534D)

Though similar to 338, the 1966 batch of AEC Reliance 6MU3RA were fitted with Weymann C49F bodywork. In use on an express service to London, the type of duties they were originally purchased for, Alder Valley 44 carries the fleet name in a non-standard position on the body side, even though the roof position is available.

Alder Valley 933 (LPF 596P), Battersea Wharf

The Bristol VRT as a dual-purpose version, as with other double-deck DP variants, was relatively uncommon in the NBC. Alder Valley operated a number of inter-urban routes into London, so a high capacity local coach version suited their particular operating requirements. 933 was in a batch of five vehicles new in 1976. Oxford, Northern and Hants & Dorset also took VRT local coaches versions.

Alder Valley 65 (LHL 246P), High Wycombe Bus Station, 13 August 1982

Transferred from Yorkshire Traction, this Alexander T-type-bodied Leyland Leopard, 1165 (LHL 256P), was originally numbered 65. Leopard 1165 was accompanied by 66 (LHL 246P) when bought, both arriving in 1982 and being renumbered that year. The bus seen here is leaving Aylesbury bus station, bound for Milton Keynes on the long-distance United Counties joint express X15 route from Reading. The Alexander-bodied vehicles were never common in Southern England NBC fleets. Alder Valley extended the depth of the white livery Yorkshire Traction had painted red up to the window line. As with many of Alder Valley dual-purpose vehicles, 1165 was later painted in red and black venetian blind livery. 1165 would later return north to serve with Grahams Coaches of Talke (Stoke-on-Trent) and Blue Bus of Horwich. (Alan Snatt)

Bristol 2147 (FHW 153D), Bristol, 1973

Views of Bristol Omnibus ECW coach-bodied Bristol MWs in NBC local coach livery use are particularly rare, probably as they only lasted a few months in this livery before withdrawal. 2147 was new to Bristol in April 1966; in 1973 it would be painted into NBC local coach livery, though it would be sold in October 1973. It found further use with independents in the North East and Dorset. Bristol had two former United Welsh, similar bodied vehicles, but with roof lights in this livery (Bristol 2135/6).

Bristol 2082 (NHW 311F), Salisbury Bus Station, 8 June 1977

With another Bristol Omnibus dual-purpose Bristol RE in the background, one could be forgiven for not realising this was a Hants & Dorset bus station. In the mid-1970s you could catch Bristol Omnibus services 241 (Trowbridge) and 270 (Bath) from Salisbury, both seen here. 2082 was slightly unusual, having a T-piece destination panel and a bus-type door. Bristol had older, similar bodied vehicles with coach doors in local coach livery. (Dave Mant)

Bristol 2057 (TAE 418G), Swindon Bus Garage, 18 July 1979

Bristol had forty-four dual-purpose RELH6L with ECW bodywork: 2041–53 DP47F coach shell (single door); 2054–78 DP49F bus shells; and 2079–84 DP45F coach shell (twin bus doors). 2057 had the early flat front; the bus-bodied batch included the later curve-fronted version as well. Freshly repainted 2057 stands at its home garage in 1979. (Dave Mant)

Bristol 2057 (TAE 418G), Swindon Bus Garage, 8 September 1985

2057 is seen again six years later, still allocated to Swindon but now in the NBC red/white local coach livery of Swindon & District; this was a local name for vehicles in the Cheltenham & Gloucester Omnibus Co., a company that had been formed from the division of Bristol in 1983. This new company applied City of Gloucester, Cheltenham District, Stroud Valleys and Swindon & District fleet names in the corporate NBC style. (Dave Mant)

Bristol 2089 (EHW 313K), Salisbury Coach Station, 16 August 1980

Delivered in 1972 in Bristol Greyhound livery as 2161, EHW 313K was a Bristol RELH6G/Plaxton Panorama Elite II C47F. It was renumbered 2089 in 1979. Note the Stroud depot prefix in front of the fleet number. With the division of Bristol Omnibus, 2089 passed to the Cheltenham & Gloucester fleet, before later being withdrawn in 1985. (Dave Mant)

Bristol 3520 (AAE 664V), Dorchester Street, Bath, *c.* 1984

Turning in front of Bath railway station, Bristol Omnibus Leyland National 2 3520 was new in June 1980 as part of a batch of thirty-five, being delivered in all-over green for bus use. Several were soon converted to dual-purpose versions for use on the X41 route to Bristol/Bath Salisbury. 3520 passed to Badgerline and retained its status in their version of 'Swiftlink' DP livery.

Crosville CVF 693 (XFM 693G), Llandudno, 1975

At a time when almost entirely made up of Bristol/ECW vehicles, in 1967 Crosville bought a batch of fourteen lightweight Bedford coaches, which were mainly allocated to Wales, probably for tour work. Painted in Crosville black and cream coach livery when new, they were all initially repainted in dual-purpose livery in 1972/73 (but not re-classed as EVF/EVT). Then, oddly, the company decided to repaint the entire batch to full NBC white coach livery soon after. CVF 693 was one of four fitted with Duple (Northern) C45F bodywork.

Crosville CVT 682 (XFM 682E), Llandudno, 1975

Seen behind CVF 693, older CVT 682 had a similar Bedford chassis, but was fitted with Duple Viscount C45F bodywork. The CVT batch totalled ten vehicles: CVT 681–686, fitted with Duple bodies, and CVT 687–90, which were completed by Plaxton.

Crosville CLL 919 (VDB 963), Cowley Road Garage, Oxford, April 1974

Caught a long way from its home garage of Northwich, CLL 919 was one of two Leyland Leopards with Plaxton bodies delivered to North Western Road Car Co. Ltd in 1963. Taken over by Crosville in 1972, they were used on contract work around Northwich, so working to Oxford was probably an unusual event. Briefly painted into Crosville black and cream coach livery and renumbered CLL 319 (ELL is correct designation), along with CLL 318 it was repainted in green/white local coach colours in 1973. Withdrawal came for both in 1975. Amazingly, VDB 963 was re-bodied with a Plaxton C53F body in April 1976, becoming LCB 924P, and found further use with a private coach operators Brabyn, Sweetin of Crosshouse and B&D travel. (Grahame Wareham)

National Bus Company Dual Purpose Vehicles 13

Crosville ELL 328 (FJA 222D), Sealand Road Workshop, Chester, March 1979

Crosville gained twelve Leyland Leopards from North Western in 1972. Ten had the attractive Alexander Y-type bodywork. Initially painted as coaches in black and cream and numbered CLL 918–929, the entire batch were painted in NBC dual-purpose livery and reclassified as ELL 318–329 in 1973. Northwich-allocated ELL 328 was seen in the snow at Crosville's central workshops in 1979, probably having been withdrawn. Four of this type had a second lease of life, being rebuilt as recovery vehicles by the company in 1975.

Crosville EPG 707 (KFM 707J), Rhyl Railway Station

One of the more unusual purchases by a NBC constituent was Crosville's 102 Seddon Pennines in 1970/71, possibly taken as other more traditional NBC types were unavailable. Crosville classified 49 as dual-purpose, though the seating only differed from the bus version in the material used. Much maligned, they were a common sight right across Crosville's vast empire, their unusual appearance only adding to Crosville's interesting fleet in the mid-1970s.

Crosville ENL 846 (NFM 846M), Crewe Garage

Crosville was the largest user of dual-purpose Leyland Nationals, owning 128, all in the 11.3-metre DP48F versions. Delivered between 1973 and 1975, some of the later deliveries had the smaller roof pod. Crosville put the first ones to work on its prestigious L1 'Cymru Coastliner' limited stop service between Chester and Caernarfon. They were ideal for Crosville, which had a huge operating area, and the comfortable seating suited many of its long rural and inter-urban services.

Crosville ELL 314 (RMA 314P), Brecon, April 1982

ELL 314 is seen at Brecon while working the long 700 'TrawsCambria' service between Bangor and Cardiff, a joint operation with National Welsh. This brought the regular sight of Crosville vehicles deep into South Wales. ELL 314 was delivered as CLL 314 to Crosville in NBC white, and was in a batch used on National Express routes between North Wales and London. In the mid-1970s Crosville, unlike other NBC constituents, did not take delivery of new coaches for dual-purpose work; only in the late 1970s did it cascade large numbers of coaches into dual-purpose livery.

Crosville ELL 29 (DDM 29X), Crewe Bus Station, 1982

Crosville's C84 service from Chester to Newcastle-under-Lyme was ideally suited to dual-purpose vehicles. Crosville used its large batch of dual-purpose Leyland Nationals on duties such as this; by the early 1980s the next generation of vehicle, such as ELL 29, could also be seen. This batch of Leyland Leopard were fitted with the troubled Willowbrook 003 bodies and were initially delivered in NBC green/white livery. Crosville returned them unused to the manufacture for rectifications. They reappeared with new registrations and in the first version of Crosville's 'Town Lynx' livery, which the company used on coach-bodied dual-purpose vehicles.

Cumberland 807 (ERM 807K), Keswick Garage

Cumberland 807 was a 1972 Ford R1014 with Duple 'Viceroy Express' C45F coachwork. In 1972, 807 received an early form of dual-purpose livery, with a central band of red. A batch of seven, they were, possibly for the bus grant allowance, repainted in red/white dual-purpose livery. Then, in the reverse to the normal pattern, received full National white coach livery. (Lindsay Young)

Cumberland 807 (ERM 807K), Coliseum Coach Station, Blackpool, 23 August 1975

Cumberland 807 is seen again now repainted in red/white local coach livery. Later, this batch would receive full National white coach livery. (Alan Snatt)

Cumberland 296 (DAO 296K)

The Cumberland fleet only operated a small number of dual-purpose vehicles in the 1970s, of which four, 296–8/600, were bus-bodied Bristol RELL6Ls (600 was a RELH6L) dating from 1971/2. By the early 1980s the company had downgraded 296–8 to buses, replacing the seats and repainting them in NBC red. In 1984, three were transferred to Bristol OC.

National Bus Company Dual Purpose Vehicles 17

Cumberland 609 (ACH 144H), Whitehaven Garage

Cumberland purchased four Leyland Leopards/Plaxton C44F from Trent in 1980. 609, seen here, was formerly Trent 44. Supplementing Cumberland's small fleet of local coaches, they were often used on contract work.

Cumberland 609 (ACH 144H), Keswick Garage

Cumberland 609 is seen again, now repainted in 'Border Clipper' livery, a scheme used for regional express services. It is unusual for an older coach to be repainted for such use. Amazingly, 609 lasted into the post-1986 Stagecoach fleet.

Cumberland 622 (VRM 622S), Workington Garage

Cumberland 622 was delivered in National white, but had been downgraded to a local coach when seen here in Workington Garage. Cumberland only ever had a handful of 'Grant-Specification' coaches.

East Kent MJG 49, London Victoria Coach Station, 6 April 1974

East Kent MJG 49 was a 1957 AEC Reliance with Beadle C41C coachwork. It is not obvious in this view, but these vehicles had a centre door, a variant unknown to the NBC in this era. Originally a batch of twelve, they had previously been in maroon and grey, East Kent keeping this attractive livery for a while longer by applying corporate lettering onto the sides. A few lasted long enough to receive full NBC local coach livery, as seen here. (Alan Snatt)

East Kent GJG 635D, London Victoria Coach Station, 1973

An East Kent Park Royal-bodied AEC Reliance delivered in 1966, GJG 635D is seen in London's Victoria coach station in 1973. Around 1972, when the corporate image was still being fully decided, companies often applied their own interpretation of dual-purpose livery. Here, East Kent have applied NBC colours and lettering, but in the same style as their previous livery. At this time East Kent did not use fleet numbers. This Park Royal-bodied combination of vehicle was rare in NBC service; Alder Valley was the only other company to have this type. United Counties obtained a number of similar vehicles from Birch Brothers, though these were on Leyland Leopard chassis. (Alan Snatt)

East Kent 1087 (NFN 87R)

East Kent and associated company Maidstone & District both took small numbers of the dual-purpose version of the ubiquitous Leyland National. East Kent took delivery of nine in 1977, including 1087, seen here. All were the long 11.3-metre version with seating for forty-eight.

East Midland C75 (275 UVO), London Victoria Coach Station, 21 April 1973

East Midland's C75 was a 1963 AEC Reliance with Willowbrook DP49F coachwork. East Midland also operated AEC Reliances with Alexander Y-type bodies in dual-purpose livery. East Midland was one of the red BET fleets to go green in NBC days. (Alan Snatt)

East Midland C91 (EVO 291J), Leicester, 1973

The only other dual-purpose variant in the East Midland fleet in the mid-1970s was the bus-bodied Bristol RE. Recently repainted into local coach livery, C91 is partway through a long journey to Luton. East Midland had a later batch of similar vehicles finished in full NBC coach white – clearly holding the bus body with coach seats in high regard!

Mansfield District MC28 (ERB 345H)

Mansfield District MC28 was a Bedford VAM70/Duple Viceroy with forty-one seats. While the corporate liveries were being decided, companies would apply their own interpretations. Mansfield District MC28 was painted in this interim dual-purpose scheme, though this livery was short-lived and this vehicle would be repainted as a full National white coach, and renumbered 228 in the joint East Midland/Mansfield numbering. It was sold in 1979 to independent owner Marsh of Macclesfield, who kept it until 1986. (Omnibus Society)

Mansfield District 12 (PRA 12R)

Fitted with the striking Alexander T-type body, Mansfield District 12 was one of a batch of six delivered to East Midland/Mansfield District. This photo predates the application of both fleet names on coaches and dual-purpose vehicles. Although Mansfield District was managed by East Midland, the fleet name never quite disappeared, thought the 'District' was dropped and just 'Mansfield' was applied before eventual privatisation. (Omnibus Society)

East Yorkshire 735 (9735 AT), Pocklington Garage, 1976

East Yorkshire operated an interesting selection of dual-purpose vehicles for a small fleet. 735 was a Leyland Leopard with a Willowbrook body. Some of this type had been painted in the dual-purpose livery but using the rare NBC blue. Withdrawn in November 1975, it is seen out of use at Pocklington Garage in 1976.

East Yorkshire 771 (9771 AT), Hull Garage, 1975

New in 1964, Leyland Leopard 771 also carried Willowbrook bodywork. Here it is seen in the snow at Hull Garage in 1975. As with a number of East Yorkshire vehicles, some of this batch had briefly carried NBC blue livery in place of the red. 771 was sold in August 1976.

National Bus Company Dual Purpose Vehicles 23

East Yorkshire 876 (RKH 876G), Blackpool Coach Park, February 1975

East Yorkshire had retained NBC blue briefly, but by the time this photo was taken in 1975 poppy red was decided to be the standard colour. Marshall-bodied Leyland Leopard 876, new in 1969, is seen here at Blackpool in 1975, a location guaranteed to have numerous interesting visiting NBC vehicles – never more so than in September, when the Illuminations were on. Later, 876 would succumb to dual-purpose red/white and was withdrawn in 1981.

East Yorkshire 922 (BKH 922K), Sheffield Bus Station, *c.* 1973

922 was one of a batch of five Leyland Leopards new in 1971 and numbered 920–924. 922 would be repainted in dual-purpose red/white, but unusually for the period had the fleet name applied centrally – a practice more common in the early 1980s. 922 would also run in National coach white.

East Yorkshire 197 (KGJ 477K)

East Yorkshire Motor Services 197, seen here working a tour of East Yorkshire villages, was a Leyland Leopard PSU5/4RT with Plaxton C57F bodywork. It was new in September 1972 to Samuelson's of London, but it had passed to United in 1978, becoming 1099. Transferred to East Yorkshire in 1980, it survived into the privatised East Yorkshire, being sold in 1987.

Eastern Counties LS791 (5791 AH), Norwich Bus Station

At the introduction of the NBC corporate livery, Eastern Counties was using just Bristol MWs and REs, both with bus-type bodies, for its dual-purpose fleet. Because of the roof lights, LS791 carries the fleet name on the side in white. Oddly, Eastern Counties applied the fleet name in the same position to a number of its other dual-purpose buses, even though the roof position was available. Maybe it could not get red transfers at the time? 'LS' was the code used for Bristol MW buses. LS591 was new as C32F in 1959 and was converted to C39F in 1969. Repainted into this NBC livery in 1973, it would be sold in 1976.

National Bus Company Dual Purpose Vehicles

Eastern Counties RLE869 (WPW 869H), Felixstowe Ferry

RLE869 is seen working route 249 along the sea at Felixstowe Ferry. Eastern Counties prefixed its vehicles' fleet numbers with identification letters: RLE indicated Bristol RE, with the addition of the letter E for dual-purpose versions. In the mid-1970s Eastern Counties was largely a Bristol/ECW fleet, with only a few exceptions. Indeed, the two 1972 grant-specification Duple Viceroy-bodied Bedford YRQs CB993/4 (VVG 538/9K) taken over from Mascot National possibly briefly carried dual-purpose livery. Eastern Counties painted its various minibuses in local coach red and white, while later seven Alexander T-types were repainted as local coaches.

Eastern National 1610 (GVW 980H), Westminster Embankment, 30 March 1977

When the corporate livery was introduced in 1972 only two Eastern National vehicles received the dual-purpose or local coach livery, Chelmsford's 1609 and 1610, seen here – both 1970 Bristol RELH6Gs with Eastern Coachworks DP47F bodies. The company downgraded this same type to full bus status at the same time, given the unusual appearance of the coach body in all-over NBC green. United and Lincolnshire would downgrade the same type to bus status some time later. (Alan Snatt)

Eastern National 1051 (TJN 974W), Battersea Coach Park, 1985

A very unusual purchase for an NBC constituent, 1051 was a 1980 Bedford YMQ/S with Wadham Stringer 'Vanguard' DP33F body – a type more commonplace with the MOD. A small batch, they lasted long enough for the privatised ENOC to use on tenders services in East London. Visible above the fleet number is the allocation plate, with 'BE' denoting Braintree – a useful addition for the enthusiast. Strangely devoid of a fleet name, this was possibly in preparation for the livery changes at this time. Today it is preserved in Eastern National privatised livery.

Eastern National 1215 (BNO 701T), London's Victoria Coach Station, 7 July 1979

Only a handful of Eastern National vehicles carried NBC dual-purpose livery. New in 1979, 1215 was a Bedford YMT with Duple Dominant II express C53F bodywork – a typical grant specification coach popular with many NBC constituents at this time. In the 1980s these vehicles and the Bedford type above, for no obvious reason, carried the fleet name lettered in two lines. (Alan Snatt)

National Bus Company Dual Purpose Vehicles

Eastern National 2200 (UCO 46L), Eastern Counties Central Workshops, Chelmsford

Eastern National's Leyland National 2200 is not what it initially appears to be. The classification dual-purpose is usually applied to a bus/coach fitted with coach seats used on longer-distance stage work, but in this case the classification applies to the ability to also be used for wheelchair access. New in 1973 to Plymouth City Transport (as No. 46), ENOC converted it in 1980 to include a central door and ramp, although it retained bus seats. It is seen here at the company's open day.

Eastern National 3067 (KOO 785V)

Eastern Counties operated express/limited stop services from Southend into London, unusually using double-deck semi-coaches. Previously using coach-seated Bristol FLFs, which were the last Lodekkas built, these were replaced by batch of Bristol VRTs equipped with powerful Gardner 6LXB engines. As with 3067, seen above, they would later be repainted in an attractive two-tone dedicated livery. In turn these VRTs would be replaced by the striking ECW Commuter coach, based on a special longer version of the Leyland Olympian and powered by the Leyland TL11 engine. 3067 would see further use with Western National.

Hants & Dorset 1005 (2691 RU), Salisbury Garage, 5 April 1975

Hants & Dorset merged with Wilts & Dorset in 1972, though they already shared many facets of operations. 1005 was previously coach 891 in the original Hants & Dorset fleet. It was converted to one-man operation and repainted into this livery in February 1974, receiving a company-made destination box as well. It would only serve for another two years before being sold to Martins of Middlewich. (Dave Mant)

Hants & Dorset 1051 (AEL 6B), Bournemouth Bus Station, 21 September 1975

Hants & Dorset repainted just two Bristol REs (1051/2) with this coach body into local coach livery, though the lack of destination indicators must have made operation on service routes difficult. Bournemouth's 1051 is seen here at the local bus station, the location where both vehicles were destroyed in the July 1976 fire, while parked in the lower deck of the coach station. (Alan Snatt)

Hants & Dorset 1024 (JEL 423E), Victoria Coach Station

Southampton-allocated 1024 (JEL 423E) was a 1967 Bristol RESH6G with Duple Northern Commander III C40F bodywork. Hants & Dorset painted numerous coach-bodied vehicles into local coach livery, including several with the unusual 'Chinese Six' twin-steer arrangement.

Hants & Dorset 3098 (AJA 148B), Salisbury Bus Station, 6 July 1976

A type more at home north of Birmingham, Hants & Dorset purchased five Leyland Leopards with Alexander Y-type bodywork from National Travel (North West) (N145–9) in 1975, though they had been new to the defunct North Western Road Car Co. in 1964. H&D numbered them 3095–9 (AJA 145–149B), allocating them to Salisbury, Bournemouth, Poole and Andover. Withdrawal would come in 1977/78. (Dave Mant)

Hants & Dorset 3091 (160 AUF), Salisbury Coach Station, 26 June 1976

Only fifteen Weymann Castilian-bodied Leyland Leopards were ever built, all for Southdown, and were new in 1962/3. Four of these vehicles were transferred to Hants & Dorset in 1973. Numbered 3091–4 (ex-Southdown 1160, 1162–4), they were re-seated from C45F to forty-nine before entry into service. Hants & Dorset allocated them to Salisbury, Southampton and Basingstoke. All were withdrawn in 1977. (Dave Mant)

Hants & Dorset 3640 (GLJ 676N), Shamrock & Rambler Garage, Bournemouth, *c.* 1980

Parked outside the Shamrock & Rambler Garage in Holdenhurst Road, 3640 is carrying white and black allocation dots for Bournemouth Garage (Norwich Avenue), which closed in November 1980. A result of the MAP Survey, the 'South Wessex' local identity was used on vehicles in East Dorset. 3640 was one of ten dual-purpose Leyland Nationals that the company bought in the years 1976–79. They would be divided between Wilts & Dorset and Hampshire Bus when the company was split.

National Bus Company Dual Purpose Vehicles

Gosport & Fareham 63 (HAM 505E), Hants & Dorset Salisbury Garage, 26 April 1975

Gosport & Fareham was more commonly known as Provincial. It operated a small but interesting fleet from its garage at Hoeford, near Fareham. Vehicles were transferred regularly from the parent fleet. Seen here, 63 was briefly with Provincial during 1975/6 – long enough to gain a Provincial number and livery. Formerly Hants & Dorset 20, it was a Bedford VAM14 with Duple Northern Viscount coachwork, and was new to Wilts & Dorset in 1967. (Dave Mant)

Gosport & Fareham 78 (XLJ 725K), Hoeford Garage, 17 July 1983

Another transfer from Hants & Dorset, Bristol RELH/ECW DP50F 78 was previously 1650 in the parent fleet. New in 1972, it had latterly operated from H&D Fareham Garage in NBC local coach red/white, carrying MAP 'New Provincial' local identity. On 31 March 1983, Gosport & Fareham was split from Hants & Dorset control and 1650 was transferred into Gosport & Fareham (Provincial) ownership. (Dave Mant)

Gosport & Fareham 1 (A301 KJT), Southampton, 23 June 1984

Provincial operated a number of Leyland Nationals in local coach livery; some were the rarer Mark 2 dual-purpose variant, though Nos 3 and 4 (C103/4 UHO) were fitted with bus seats. Nos 1 and 2 (A301/2 KJT) were true dual-purpose vehicles. No. 1 is seen here leaving Southampton bus station in 1984 on a service suited to these vehicles – the X16 limited stop to Southsea. (Dave Mant)

Hants & Dorset 3347 (NJT 47P), Salisbury Bus Station, 26 June 1982

Hants & Dorset were one of the few fleets to use double-deck local coaches. 3347 was from a batch of six that were new in 1977. Hants & Dorset was a keen user of local identities, being formed as a result of MAP (Market Analysis Project) activities. 'Antonbus' was applied to Andover-based vehicles, named after the River Anton that runs through the town. The 208 service is a rare survivor in today's decimated rural routes and is still operated as the 'Active 8', being run jointly by Wilts & Dorset and Stagecoach. (Dave Mant)

National Bus Company Dual Purpose Vehicles 33

Hants & Dorset 1061 (WEL 464J), Basingstoke Garage

Hants & Dorset operated a fascinating fleet – possibly the most varied in the NBC empire. It had an amazing number of different dual-purpose vehicles, not being afraid of small numbers. Leyland Leopard 1061 had been in National white coach livery, like 1062 alongside, and in the manner of things had naturally downgraded to red/white DP livery. Hants & Dorset used coloured dots to indicate the vehicle area/garage – in this case a blue dot indicated the northern area (Salisbury), while a black dot indicated Basingstoke Garage.

Wilts & Dorset 3903 (A903 JPR), Bristol Bus Station, 6 July 1976

The government dictated that larger NBC companies would be broken up, apparently to make sales more attractive, so with the division of Hants & Dorset, the Wilts & Dorset name reappeared after an absence of eleven years, the remainder becoming Hampshire Bus. 3903 was one of five ECW-bodied Leyland Olympians with coach seating bought by the newly divided company for limited stop routes from Salisbury. It is seen on the 786 from Bristol to Portsmouth, standing in for a National Express coach – an action possible when we had one state-owned bus company. The passengers no doubt welcomed the seats.

London Country RP7 (JPA 107K)

When London Country was established in January 1970 it had no coaches, and although it operated the Green Line services as limited stop coach services, the vehicles – apart from fourteen 1964-bought AEC Reliance vehicles (RC class) – were in most cases hardly distinguishable from ordinary buses. In an attempt to cut costs by using one-man operated vehicles, the company bought another ninety AEC Reliances, this time with Park Royal bodies (RP class) for Green Line work, displacing the Routemasters as they were more reliable. With the introduction of the corporate livery, Green Line vehicles were painted in standard dual-purpose livery. Despite their issues, the RPs survived on local work across the Home Counties.

London Country SMA 1 (JPF 101K), Crawley Bus Station, 14 September 1978

SMA 1 was part of a batch of twenty-one AEC Swifts with stylish Alexander W-type bodies, originally intended for South Wales Transport. However, under the auspices of the NBC they were diverted to LCBS to ease the company's fleet issues. This form of Alexander bodywork was never popular south of the border, and even less so with the NBC, in which the local coach version was unique to London Country. Newly formed London Country suffered many vehicle issues in the 1970s and not all the SMA class lasted long enough to be repainted into corporate livery. Utilised on the 725 Gravesend–Windsor cross-London service, until being replaced by the new RB/RS coaches, SMA 1 was reallocated to Crawley, being demoted to bus work until its withdrawal in 1978.

National Bus Company Dual Purpose Vehicles

London Country SNC 34 (XPD 234N), Central London, *c.* 1975

Through the mid-1970s, London Country purchased sixty-two 'suburban coach' Leyland Nationals to ease its vehicle problems. Both long (11.3 metre) and short (10.3 metre) versions in local coach livery were taken into the fleet, though the early deliveries were fitted with bus seats. SNC 34 (**S**hort **N**ational **C**oach), new in 1974, unusually carries a black and silver registration plate.

London Country RB19 (PPH 449R)

Previously relying on Leyland Nationals and a number of older AEC Reliances, London Country decided to revitalise its Green Line network in the mid-1970s, eventually using 150 grant-specification coaches in a modified Green Line livery. The first vehicles were thirty AEC Reliances with bodywork by either Duple Dominant (the RB class) or Plaxton Supreme (the RS class). The two classes were numbered into a common sequence. These coaches were acquired new in 1977 on a five-year lease from Kirby Central, and they helped to reverse the decline of Green Line brand. Being supplemented by many more similar vehicles over the next few years, they became a familiar sight on the capital's roads.

Lincolnshire 1652 (GVL 908F), Newark Bus Station, 1975

Lincolnshire was a large user of the Bristol LH/ECW type, including the rare dual-purpose version, of which it was the largest user in the NBC with twenty-four. Among the NBC, the early flat-fronted version in the dual-purpose variation was unique to Lincolnshire Road Car Co. 1652 was one of six originally delivered in 1968 with shallow windscreens, although these were soon rebuilt by ECW. 1652, still with an early plain green 'double N' symbol, was caught at Newark bus station in the mid-1970s. The batch of twenty-four included some with updated fronts, which in dual-purpose mode would only be found elsewhere in the NBC in very small numbers, such as Eastern Counties and United, and even those were re-seated conversions.

Lincolnshire 2240 (PFE 717K), Southwell, August 1981

Less unusual is 2240 (originally numbered 1240), which was one of a batch of seven Bristol RELH6G/ECW DP47F delivered in 1970. When new in 1973 this batch was painted in full National white coach livery, which was unusual but not unique. Cumberland, East Midland, Eastern Counties and United Counties also painted bus-bodied Bristol REs as coaches; Lincolnshire also had several earlier Bristol REs with ECW coach bodies in local coach livery. 2240 is seen in Southwell (Nottinghamshire).

Maidstone & District 2816 (OKO 816G)

A classic Maidstone & District vehicle, 2816 was a Leyland Leopard fitted with Willowbrook DP49F bodywork and a standard BET body, and hailed from a batch of eighteen delivered in 1968. 2816 was used for staff transport from September 1981, and in 1984 entered preservation, where it survived in its original M&D green and cream livery.

Maidstone & District 2806 (OKO 806G), Forest Row, East Sussex

Maidstone & District 2806 is calling at Forest Row in East Sussex while working the 291 service from Crawley to Tunbridge Wells. A Willowbrook-bodied Leyland Leopard, it is from the same batch as 2816 above.

Maidstone & District 2853 (LJH 253L), Eastbourne, 28 May 1975

Looking similar to other BET-bodied M&D dual-purpose vehicles, 2853 (LJH 253L), a 1973 Leyland PSU3B/2R Leopard with Willowbrook DP51F coachwork, was one of two acquired with the business of Dengate of Rye. The takeover of Dengate bought three other interesting DP vehicles into the M&D fleet: Leyland Leopards 2854/5 (2854 shown below) and an unusual Willowbrook 001-bodied Ford R192, 3244 (SNM 244J), which was one of only three to carry dual-purpose livery in the NBC, and the only one to carry NBC DP green/white. (Jeremy Chapter)

Maidstone & District 2854 (LJH 254L), London Victoria Coach Station, 7 June 1980

Maidstone & District 2854 (LJH 254L), a 1973 Leyland PSU3B/4R Leopard with Plaxton 'Panorama Elite III' express C49F coachwork, was taken over with the business of Dengate of Rye in 1974. M&D converted it to dual-purpose use and re-seated it to DP53F. It survived with M&D until 1985. (Alan Snatt)

National Bus Company Dual Purpose Vehicles

Maidstone & District 3910 (SKN 910R), London's Victoria Coach Station, 7 July 1979

Carrying mismatched Hastings & District fleet names, Maidstone & District 3910 (SKN 910R) was a 1977 Leyland National I, Series A, 11.3-metre DP48F. Though fitted with high-backed seats, it would not have been as comfortable as the coach-bodied dual-purpose vehicles then becoming available. The later Leyland National was built with the smaller roof pod. Maidstone & District operated eleven dual-purpose Leyland Nationals.

Maidstone & District 2162 (JKK 162V), Victoria Coach Station

2162, a Leyland Leopard with Duple Dominant body, was built to grant specifications. This was a very popular type with the NBC at the time. With the local identity carried on separate panels, this vehicle would receive full NBC venetian blind livery with 'Invictaway' lettering. Later, some of this batch received the striking black and red diagonal band version of the Invictaway branding.

Maidstone & District 2113 (JKE 113L), July 1985

As Maidstone & District expanded its network into London and Gatwick from Maidstone and the Medway towns, it used downgraded coaches for the new services. 2113 was a 1973 Leyland Leopard PSU3B/4R/Duple Dominant C44F, previously numbered 4113. M&D numbered its vehicles according to use, with the 2xxx series indicating dual-purpose. 2113 is seen in July 1985, soon after it was repainted in the NBC venetian blind livery with Invictaway branding.

Midland Red 5794 (CHA 94C), Oxford Gloucester Green Bus Station, August 1973

Like Crosville, Midland Red had a degree of confusion when painting its dual-purpose vehicles. Some of this batch of forty-nine (classed LC7 by MROC) were painted NBC white and then red/white before being repainted back into National white. 5794, a 1965 Leyland PSU3/4R with Duple Northern 'Commander II' C49F coachwork, passed to National Travel (South West) in National white in December 1975. After sale from the NBC, it was used by number of Bristol coach operators, one of which, Crown Coaches, re-bodied it in 1981 with a Plaxton Supreme IV body, and reregistered it FTC 2W. (Grahame Wareham)

Midland Red 5856 (JHA 856E)

An extremely rare view of one of the Midland Red home-built vehicles in local coach livery. Midland Red 5856 (JHA 856E) was a 1967-built BMMO S19 with a DP49F body. Although clearly a dual-purpose vehicle, the company only painted two into the appropriate livery, and both were repainted almost immediately. The NBC had certain rules over vehicle age and demotion to bus use – perhaps these vehicles fell foul of corporate directive? (Omnibus Society)

Midland Red 204 (JHA 204L), Cheltenham Coach Station

When Midland Red ceased construction of its own vehicles it became a large user of the Leyland Leopard with Marshall Bodywork, in both bus and dual-purpose configurations. In a batch of fifty (Midland Red type code SDP27) 204 was new in February 1973. With the break-up of Midland Red in September 1981, 204 passed to Midland Red (West) Ltd. Withdrawal came in August 1985, though it languished at Worcester Garage until December 1987, when it was sold to Passenger Vehicle Spares (Barnsley) Ltd. Midland Red operated 152 vehicles with this body in dual-purpose livery.

Midland Red 2146 (WUX 656K), Heath Hayes Garage

The 1970s takeovers of the independent operators Harpers, Coopers and Green Bus brought a number of non-standard vehicles into the MROC fleet. One such vehicle was 2146, a Bedford YRQ with a Duple Viceroy Express C45F body. One of a pair (the other was 2147, XUX 558K), both were ex-Cooper & Sons of Oakengates. Being fitted with a 'grant doors', Midland Red painted them in DP livery. They were sold in 1977/78 respectively.

Midland Red 441 (VPF121M), Evesham, 1977

In May 1977 Midland Red acquired three Ford Transit minibuses from London County that had previously been used for a Harlow Dial-a-Ride service in a green and white livery. All had B16F bodywork by Dormobile, and on passing to Midland Red they were allocated the type code M1 and repainted to red and white NBC dual-purpose livery. 441 (later 2121) was one of two allocated to Evesham depot for the new 'Wayfarer' network of services, while the third entered service at Redditch depot for revisions to the 'Reddibus' network of services. Initially these three vehicles had the fleet numbers 441–3, but in September 1977 the three minibuses were renumbered 2121, 2124 and 2123, and were joined by an additional two identical minibuses, which were numbered 2122 and 2125. Not entirely successful, Midland Red soon replaced them with twenty-seven-seat, shortened Ford R192/Plaxton midibuses. Some of the Ford Transit minibuses found further use at Midland Red as ancillary vehicles.

National Bus Company Dual Purpose Vehicles

Midland Red East 610 (VYM 505M), Victoria Coach Station

Leyland Leopard 610 had an interesting history. Purchased new by National Travel (South East) in April 1974, by April 1979 it was transferred to Cumberland, and then in April 1982 it passed to Midland Red (East) who later renumbered it 2610 and painted it the red/yellow Midland Express livery.

Midland Red West 675 (SOA 675S), Worcester Bus Station

Midland Red was broken up into five companies by government dictate, with the four resulting companies being prefixed by the points of the compass. Though operating as separate companies, common sense showed that the joint local limited stop network would benefit from one identity – ironically, what they'd already had as one company! The distinctive Midland Express livery was therefore applied to many dual-purpose vehicles from all four companies. New in 1977, 675 was from a batch of eighteen vehicles classed as C18 (later CDP18), and these carried NBC red/white local coach livery from new. 675 was repainted into this Midland Express livery in February 1984, and withdrawal came in 1993. Along with a similar type, 675 is seen at Worcester bus station in the mid-1980s while working the hourly X93 service running between Birmingham, Kidderminster and Worcester.

National Bus Company Dual Purpose Vehicles

Northern General 5000 (PCN 9), Rigby Road Depot, Blackpool

Northern General 5000 (PCN 9), a 1963 AEC Reliance with Plaxton 'Panorama' C41F coachwork in NBC local coach livery, was originally numbered 2609. Northern General had a number of these older types and Harrington Grenadier coaches that it painted in dual-purpose livery. 5000 is seen alongside Blackpool Corporation's Rigby Road depot, adjacent to the Coliseum coach station – a well-known gathering point for NBC vehicles in the mid-1970s. (Alan Snatt)

Northern General 4182 (HCN 8G), Coliseum Coach Station, Blackpool

Again at Blackpool, Northern General 4182 is a 1969 Leyland Leopard PSU3A/4R Alexander C47F. These vehicles were popular with the Northern General Group.

National Bus Company Dual Purpose Vehicles   45

Northern General 5037 (MCN 886L), Cowley Road Garage, Oxford, July 1975

Northern General 5037, a Bristol RELH/ECW, is seen at the unlikely location of Cowley Road Garage, Oxford, in July 1975. It appears to be working a long-distance duty and possibly requires attention or fuel. This batch was delivered in 1972 in a pre-corporate livery of red/cream with the fleet name in large red letters. Northern painted them into this variation on the dual-purpose scheme with more white, though later they would be repainted with the more familiar proportions of red to white. Only Trent and Northern downgraded this type to bus status. 5037, renumbered 4886, was later painted all-over yellow. (Grahame Wareham)

Northern General 5016 (DCN 6D), Philadelphia Garage

Previously in National white and numbered 2626, Leyland Leopard/Plaxton 5016 had been repainted into dual-purpose livery by the time it was seen at Northern's Philadelphia Garage. Evidence can be seen in the windscreen of use to the popular destination of Blackpool.

Northern General 5073 (TUP 573V), Battersea Coach Park

Northern took delivery of the Willowbrook-bodied Leyland Leopard in both coach and dual-purpose liveries. Basically the same vehicle, both had grant-style opening double doors. Delivered in 1982, 5073 appears new when photographed in Battersea coach park. It survived into the privatised era with Go-Ahead Northern.

Venture 291 (RUP 291K)

Northern General 291 is seen on excursion work in Scarborough. Carrying Venture fleet names, it displays the modified front fitted to later-build Alexander Y-type bodies. Northern General had a number of subsidiary fleets, of which Venture and Tynemouth had vehicles lettered and painted in the dual-purpose livery. Eventually Northern dropped its sub-fleet names. (Omnibus Society)

National Bus Company Dual Purpose Vehicles

Northern General (SUP 205E), Blackpool, 1973

Bedford VAM14 SUP 205E, built in 1967 with Duple Viceroy C45F bodywork, was part of a batch of six originally owned by the Venture Transport Co. (Newcastle) Ltd, and was given the fleet number VC5. The company was taken over on 1 May 1970 and became part of the Northern General Transport Co. Ltd, though the fleet name was retained even into the corporate era. SUP 205E was purchased in November 1974 by Lloyds of Bagillt, lasting with them until 1982.

Northern General 4346 (GFT 805G) and 4345 (EFT 704F)

Two Leyland Leopard/Alexander Y-types, both carrying Tynemouth fleet names. 4346, nearest the camera, was Tynemouth 305, while 4345 was 304. Note how the fleet name is carried below the windows – a practice not unusual to Northern Group DP vehicles. Both of these would eventually carry Northern fleet names and be downgraded to buses in all-over yellow – the colour applied to NBC vehicles operating in the Tyne & Wear PTE region. (Omnibus Society)

Oxford South Midland 2 (DFC 602D)

Possibly at Alder Valleys Reading Garage, City of Oxford 2 was a 1966 AEC Reliance with Duple Northern 'Commander II' C49F coachwork. Along with 1 (DFC 601D), these vehicles had been in National white until 1974, when they were downgraded to local coach work. Oxford South Midland had a small but fascinating fleet with numerous dual-purpose vehicles, using both bus and coach-bodied types.

Oxford South Midland 21 (LJB 421E)

City of Oxford 21 (LJB 421E) was a Bristol RELH6G/ECW DP47F that was new in May 1967 to Thames Valley (numbered 421). 21 had come to COMS in 1971, when the Oxford–London coach operator South Midland, which had been controlled by the neighbouring Thames Valley Traction company, was transferred to City of Oxford Motors. The fleet name for the amalgamated operation became Oxford South Midland. (Lindsay Young)

Oxford South Midland 47 (RTJ 364G), Gloucester Green Bus Station, Oxford

Oxford South Midland initially loaned and then purchased two Plaxton C45F coach-bodied Ford R192s from Midland Red in 1974. RTJ 364G and AAW 471K had been acquired by Midland Red with the business of Hoggins of Wrockwardine Wood in the same year. Though allocated numbers 2180/81, they never operated either vehicle, loaning them to Oxford instead, who numbered them 47/48 respectively. Acquired in 1975, they lasted until Oxford withdrew both in July 1979. They both lasted a little longer with independents Fleetville, Cheshunt (RTJ 364G) and Garnham, Woodbridge (AAW 471K). (Lindsay Young)

Oxford South Midland 60 (VNT 848J)

Bedford YRQs with Willowbrook DP45F bodies, 59 (UUJ 447J) and 60 (VNT 848J) were loaned and then sold by Midland Red as 47/48 above, though these two had come to Midland Red from G. Cooper & Sons, Oakengates, in 1973. Midland Red numbered them 2144/45 and they were used briefly by Wellington Garage from October 1973 until January 1974, when they moved to Oxford South Midland, who disposed of them in 1978 to independent operators. (Lindsay Young)

Oxford South Midland 18 (KKV 800G), Wolvercote, Oxford, March 1974

KKV 800G was a 1968 Daimler Roadliner SRP8 single-deck demonstrator with Plaxton Derwent fifty-three seat, dual-purpose bodywork. It came to Oxford in 1970, initially numbered 639. It carried a number of liveries, the second of which was the fleet's first application of ivory and maroon with Oxford South Midland fleet names. Renumbered at this point to 18, it eventually received corporate livery, as seen here. It suffered reliability problems and was sold for scrap to Barraclough's (Carlton) in August 1976. The Plaxton Derwent in the dual-purpose version was uncommon in the NBC, other users being West Riding, South Wales, United and later Ribble, who operated small numbers. (Grahame Wareham)

Oxford South Midland 19 (436 GAC), Cowley Road Garage, Oxford, June 1974

Though Wessex National (Black & White) operated four examples in National white, Oxford 19 was unique to the NBC in the corporate era. Formerly with Midland Red (2055) and earlier, Stratford Blue (55/59), it was a 1963 Leyland Leopard PSU3/3R with the unusual Duple Northern Alpine Continental C49F bodywork. It had come to Oxford in February 1973 and initially ran in all-over red, possibly Midland Red's livery, with the Oxford South Midland name applied. Around 1973, the company repainted it in the dual-purpose colours. Withdrawal came in April 1975. (Grahame Wareham)

National Bus Company Dual Purpose Vehicles 51

Oxford South Midland 49 (SWL 49J), Farringdon Garage, June 1974

Illustrating not every vehicle in the Oxford South Midland was unusual, 49 was a standard Willowbrook BET style-bodied vehicle, though on an AEC Reliance 505 chassis. Oxford had a batch of seven, dating from 1971. Later, 49 would be repainted with the amount of white extended deeper in line with the windscreen, before eventually being downgraded to a bus and renumbered 749. Disposed of by Oxford in 1980, it passed through a number of north Staffordshire independents, including the well-known operator Berresfords of Cheddleton. (Grahame Wareham)

PMT 17 (LVT 117K), *c.* 1974

Potteries Motor Traction 17 was a Ford R226 with Plaxton Panorama Elite III C49F bodywork. PMT applied corporate fleet names to the pre-corporate livery on a number of its coaches – not strictly a local coach livery, but an interesting variation.

PMT 162 (BEH 162H), Rigby Road Tram Depot, Blackpool, 9 August 1975

Potteries Motor Traction 162 (BEH 162H), a 1970 AEC Reliance with Alexander Y-type DP49F coachwork, is seen in NBC local coach livery alongside the tram depot next to the Coliseum coach station in Blackpool. A typical PMT dual-purpose vehicle, 162 features the early front styling. It bears a potentially misleading destination blind, as this is not returning, as one would imagine, to Newcastle-under-Lyme, but its namesake in the North East. (Alan Snatt)

PMT 211 (MVT 211K), Uttoxeter Bus Station

Potteries used the Bristol RE/ECW in various lengths and door combinations for its buses, but just three were fitted with dual-purpose bodywork (210–2). Seen in Uttoxeter bus station about to work the X38 to Cheadle, all three had the single piece rear window and boot space below.

National Bus Company Dual Purpose Vehicles

PMT 37 (XEH 137M), Blackpool Coach Park, October 1977

Previously using mainly AEC Reliance/Alexander Y-types for its local coaches, by the mid-1970s Potteries Motor Traction (PMT) increased its dual-purpose fleet with the addition of Duple-bodied 'grant coaches'. Potteries 37, a Ford R1014/Duple DP41F, is seen on excursion duties at the ever-popular destination of Blackpool, though it would probably spend most of its time on inter-urban services between the Six Towns.

PMT 311 (GTX 762W), Hanley, 11 October 1987

The registration gives this little vehicle away as not being a Potteries native. Indeed, PMT 311 – a Bristol LHS fitted with ECW body in the rare DP27F configuration – was formerly National Welsh MD8027 (GTX 762W), new in February 1981. National Welsh had a total of nine of these. A pair, comprising 311 and 310 (GTX 760W), went to PMT in the mid-1980s. 311 survives today preserved in this livery but with National Welsh lettering. Other dual-purpose NBC versions of the LHS served with Alder Valley and Southern Vectis.

Ribble 929 (FCK 929F)

Ribble always had a reputation for a high-quality finish to their fleet and Leyland Leopard 923 is a fine example. Fitted with Willowbrook DP49F bodywork, these vehicles had a striking appearance; the double lights made them look quite different from the single light bus version of this body. This was the most common dual-purpose type in the Ribble fleet and this BET body style was supplied by a number of different manufactures. (Omnibus Society)

Ribble 1071 (NJA 314G), Blackpool Bus Station

Ribble's other non-coach-bodied dual-purpose type was a batch of five Alexander Y-types that had come from North Western Road Car when the company was broken up in 1973. Interestingly, some were refitted with differing front panels from newer Alexander Y-types and 1068 (NJA 311G), uniquely for the NBC, had the front from this type when fitted to a Bristol chassis.

National Bus Company Dual Purpose Vehicles 55

Ribble 1021 (PTF 716L), Carlisle, 27 August 1977

Ribble, along with Trent, Northern and Alder Valley, took the delivery of the redesigned ECW coach body in the local coach livery from new. Ribble 1021 was new in 1972 as part of a batch of ten, and would later receive green/white dual-purpose livery when it was transferred to Crosville, becoming Macclesfield Garage's ERL 528 in 1982.

Ribble 1032 (XTF 806L), Blackpool Coliseum Coach Station

Ribble's 1034, a Leyland Leopard/Duple Dominant, was really just a downgraded coach in dual-purpose livery, fitted with a single-leaf door and a small destination panel. Delivered in the same year as 1021, it is interesting to see the different approach to styling between the two companies. From a batch of thirty-two, these vehicles started life in National white with Ribble lettering, as opposed to Standerwick, which the company had a long association with until the name disappeared, becoming part of National Travel North West in 1974. (Alan Snatt)

South Wales 210 (KKG 210F), Neath Garage, 13 May 1982

210 was an AEC Reliance 6MU3R/Marshall DP41F purchased new by Western Welsh (210) in August 1967, and transferred to South Wales Transport in 1972. From a batch numbered 201–215, three were converted to towing vehicles (204/9/15) by the company in the early 1980s.

South Wales 153 (567 ECY), Swansea, 29 March 1975

South Wales 153 (567 ECY) was a 1963 AEC Reliance with Harrington Cavalier C51F bodywork. Originally a 'Brown Bomber' in the famous Neath & Cardiff Luxury Coaches fleet, four of this type came to South Wales Transport (151–4) in December 1970. (Alan Snatt)

National Bus Company Dual Purpose Vehicles 57

South Wales 173 (UNY 832G) and 460 (UCY 979J), Gorseinon Garage

In NBC days South Wales had an interesting and varied fleet. Here is another ex-Neath & Cardiff Luxury Coaches AEC Reliance, No. 173, featuring Plaxton C51F bodywork. In the background is another ex-N&C AEC, 460 – one of two 1970 Plaxton Derwent dual-purpose examples delivered just before takeover by South Wales Transport. (Andrew Tucker)

South Wales 221 (PWM 221M)

Again illustrating the variety in the SWT fleet in the 1970s, the Willowbrook 'Expressway' body was unique among NBC fleets. It bought two batches between 1973 and 1975: nine on the Bedford YRQ chassis with forty-five seats, as seen on 221 above, and four on the longer Bedford YRT chassis, seating fifty-one. Oddly, the company would paint some of the YRQs into National Express white before disposing of them in 1981.

South Wales 501 (WCY 211E)

Gorseinon Garage's Bristol RE displays a modified form of local coach livery. One of a pair new in 1967 to neighbouring United Welsh (53), a fleet which was absorbed by South Wales in 1971, 501 had previously been in standard local coach livery as 165. It was re-instated to work a park and ride contact, and was also painted in National coach white.

South Wales 471 (HCY 471N)

Reverting to something more conventional, South Wales bought grant Duple Dominant Express buses on AEC Reliance and Leyland Leopards chassis in 1975–77. A regular sight connecting South Wales towns and cities, some would be branded for the joint 'ExpressWest' services between towns from Haverfordwest to Bristol. Oddly, 471 would be renumbered 163 and repainted in National white in the early 1980s.

National Bus Company Dual Purpose Vehicles

South Wales 281 (FCY 281W)

An unusual purchase for an NBC constituent, 281 was a Bedford YMQ/Duple DP45F new in October 1980. Seen here, it displays the last version of the local coach livery before privatisation. SWT also painted some of its grant coaches in this livery. After withdrawal in 1988, it found use locally with D-Coaches of Morriston. (West Wales)

Southdown 461 (PUF 161H), Portsmouth Garage

Delivered in 1969, Southdown's 461 was one of twenty-nine Leyland Leopards in a rare – and unique in the NBC – combination with Northern Counties DP49F bodies. When the corporate image was introduced in 1972, these were the only vehicles to receive dual-purpose livery in the Southdown fleet. For a large operating area it is interesting that Southdown had such a small fleet of dual-purpose vehicles. Later, a number of the downgraded coaches and grant-specification coaches would be painted in green/white dual-purpose livery.

Southdown 3004 (LCD 242F), Portsmouth Winston Churchill Avenue

Southdown downgraded three of its Leyland Leopards/Plaxton Panorama C49F, 3003/4/7 (originally numbered 1241/2/5) all were allocated to Portsmouth for contact work. 3004 is seen on Winston Churchill Avenue alongside Southdown's Portsmouth garage, if the destination is correct, is preparing for a long journey. The re-numbering into the 3xxx series was for fully depreciated vehicles.

Southdown 1288 (RYJ 888R), Pool Valley Bus Station, Brighton

Southdown's first coaches to receive NBC dual-purpose livery was a 1977 batch of nine Leyland Leopard PSU3E/4Rs with grant-specification Duple Dominant bodywork. Locally allocated 1288 stands at Pool Valley bus station when about to work the service 'Sealine 773' to Gatwick.

Southdown 1316 (ANJ 316T), Battersea Coach Park

Following on from the batch above, Southdown's purchased thirteen Leyland Leopard local coaches in 1978, this time with Plaxton Supreme Express bodywork. Portsmouth-allocated 1316 lays over after working the 075 National Express service from its home city. Southdown repainted this vehicle into National Express white in the early 1980s.

Southern Vectis 204 (KDL 204W), Newport Bus Station, 16 June 1983

With its obvious geographic constraints, Southern Vectis did not operate local coaches until 1981, when it purchased three Bristol LHS6Ls with Eastern Coachworks DP33F bodywork. These three Bristol LHS6Ls had the distinction of being the only Southern Vectis vehicles painted in NBC corporate dual-purpose livery, apart from open-top buses and the company's service vans. Seen here, Southern Vectis 204 (KDL 204W) is wearing NBC local coach livery at Newport bus station. 204 eventually crossed to the mainland with Solent Blue Line and found further service with a number of Dorset independents, namely Blandford Bus Co., Shaftesbury & District and Cudlipp (Linco Travel). (Alan Snatt)

Trent 216 (216 ACH), Derby Garage, 1976

Trent 216 was a Leyland Leopard/Willowbrook DP51F, new April 1963. A long-serving dual-purpose vehicle, at this age it would be usual to downgrade it to bus use, but possibly Trents' 1976 Derby Garage fire affected the fleet usage? These vehicles were originally painted in an attractive red and cream livery that followed the trim still visible under the red paint. Trent had an eclectic fleet of BET-bodied vehicles and later ECW types as a number of vehicles came from Midland General when that fleet was absorbed in the mid-1970s, and like many fleets it added grant-specification coach-bodied Duples and Plaxtons when the government scheme was introduced.

Trent 241 (ECH 241C), Marble Arch, London, 17 April 1976

Trent 241 (ECH 241C), a 1965 Leyland PSU3/1R Leopard with Willowbrook DP49F bodywork in NBC local coach livery, is seen in central London in 1976. NBC management frowned upon the use of dual-purpose vehicles on services into Victoria coach station, preferring the unified image of the white National coach network, which the corporate image was designed for. 241 would be sold by Trent in 1978 to West Wales Motors, Tycroes, in South Wales. (Alan Snatt)

Trent 97 (TCH 97L) 203 (203CCH), Derby Garage, September 1973

Trent painted a number of its coaches in this interim livery in 1972/3, but all would be repainted into National white soon after. A Bedford YRQ /Duple C41F, Trent 97 was a new in 1973 so was probably delivered in this livery. Seen standing alongside is Trent 203 – a Leyland Leopard with Willowbrook DP51F bodywork. Just visible in front of the fleet number is the depot allocation code BN (indicating Buxton).

Trent 287 (ORC 416N), Sheffield Bus Station, 7 August 1985

Seen here, 287 was a 1974 Bristol RELH6G/ECW DP49F. In a batch of twenty-one bought between 1972 and 1974, the bus body was fitted to seventeen, of which twelve were allocated to Midland General, the remainder being allocated to Trent from new. The Midland General name was lost in 1976 when its vehicles were fully absorbed into the Trent fleet. 287 waits to depart from Sheffield Pond Street bus station with the 256 service to Ripley. 287 would finish it days in the North East with 'Catch a Bus'.

Trent 107 (YCH 897M), Sheffield Bus Station

Nottingham Garage's Trent 107, hailing from a batch of seven (101–7, ex-150/1/3–7) new in April 1974, was a Bristol RE fitted with the comparatively rare ECW DP47F body. This batch was delivered in local coach livery, but 107 would later be painted into unrelieved NBC bus red at Langley Mill Garage. It is seen here loading at Sheffield Pond Street bus station with the X53 service to Nottingham. In the background is an East Midland Bristol VRT.

Trent 128 (UVO 128S), Derby Bus Station

Seen about to work to Burton-on-Trent, Derby Garage's 128 was a 1977 Leyland Leopard with a Duple grant-specification C49F body. Trent took delivery of both Duple and Plaxton local coaches in this year.

Trent 109 (PRA 109R), Wembley Stadium

Trent, like the three other East Midland NBC constituents, took delivery of the Alexander T-type in dual-purpose configuration, though only Trent painted them as coaches in National white. Trent's 109 was on a Leyland Leopard chassis, delivered in 1976, part of a batch of eight, it was allocated to Derby garage. All survived into the deregulated era. Today 109 survives preserved in the yellow and blue colours of its last owner, Whites of Calver, part of the former Chesterfield Transport. (Alan Snatt)

Midland General 73 (ERB 343H)

Midland General 73 was a Bedford VAM70/Duple Viceroy. As Mansfield MC28 (shown earlier) it carried an interim dual-purpose livery, and in the same fashion was then repainted as a white National coach. Briefly a 'blue' NBC constituent, Midland General was absorbed by Trent, although the name remained in use in NBC poppy red livery until 1976. ERB 343H was one of two transferred to West Yorkshire in 1977.

Midland General 232 (LNU 344J), Sheffield Pond Street Bus Station, 1973

Delivered in 1971, 232 was a Bedford YRQ with a Plaxton C41F body. These were delivered in cream livery and originally had a black relief at waist height, and boasted Mansfield District/ Midland General joint fleet names. They were later changed to blue with NBC-style Midland General fleet names, as seen here. A batch of four, all were transferred to West Yorkshire in 1977, with 232 (by then Trent 88) becoming their 2103. All retained the National coach white that they were repainted into soon after this photo was taken. (Transport Library)

Midland General 137 (BNN 103C), Victoria Bus Station, Nottingham

New in 1965 to Mansfield District, Bristol MW 137 was transferred to Midland General in 1968. Illustrating the confused vehicle history of the NBC companies in Derbyshire and Nottinghamshire, 137 was then transferred to Trent in October 1976, lasting with them until withdrawal in August 1977. Some of Midland General's earlier Bristol MWs were transferred to Trent in 1973, being repainted into full NBC dual-purpose livery with Trent fleet names.

Midland General 266 (1385R), Ilkeston Garage

Bristol RELH6G/ECW DP51F 266 was new to Midland General in 1964. The company had three of these vehicles – 1384R–6R (originally 30–32, later 130–132). 266 was fitted opening vent windows, an unusual feature on this body style, while 265 (1384R) and 267 (1386R) had fixed windows and were painted in National coach white. Transferred to Trent in January 1977, 266 retained local coach livery, but it was withdrawn in September 1977 after only nine months with Trent.

Midland General 134 (371 RNN), Grantham Bus Station

Looking superb in freshly painted poppy red and white, Midland General 134 was a thirty-nine-seat Bristol MW/ECW of 1963. Originally lettered in the joint Midland General/Mansfield district fleet as 288, it was downgraded in 1971. Although taken over by Trent in October 1976, it is unlikely 134 received their fleet name as it was withdrawn in the November. Still in use at this time was the very small depot code just visible in front of the fleet number – LM indicating Langley Mill. (Transport Library)

Midland General 133 (SRB 66F), Matlock Bus Station

At first sight a standard Bristol RE, 133 was actually a Bristol RESH6G. The RESH (33-foot-high frame) version of the RE was a rare vehicle, most being bodied as coaches by Duple, and just two having ECW bodies. Midland General had both vehicles, allocating them to Mansfield for their working lives. 133 would later become Trent 145, and is seen alongside Trent 107 (HRC 107C), a dual-purpose Alexander Y-type C41F with a Leyland Tiger Cub chassis. (Omnibus Society)

Midland General 280 (TCH 280L)

Midland General had a batch of Bristol RELH6Ls fitted with ECW DP49F bodies. All were transferred Trent in 1976. 280 was later painted unrelieved poppy red, though retained its high-backed seating. It was sold by Trent in July 1990.

National Bus Company Dual Purpose Vehicles

Midland General 113 (PRA 113R), Mount Street Bus Station, Nottingham, 1977

113 is one of a batch of eight Leyland Leopards with Alexander T-type bodies. These were the last vehicles delivered lettered 'Midland General' before the fleet was fully integrated with Trent. Lasting into privatisation, the whole batch (PRA 108–115R) passed to Lancaster City Transport, and 113 was then used by a number of independents before being cut down for use as a towing vehicle. (Omnibus Society)

United 1100 (910 THN)

An extremely rare view of a United Bristol MW/ECW in local coach livery. 910 THN was unusual in that it started life in 1962 as forty-five-seat bus (BU710) before conversion in 1965 to DP39F (UE710). It carried the United's classic olive green livery with Thames–Tees–Tyne fleet names. Repainted in dual-purpose livery in November 1974, it finished service at Hartlepool as 2790 in February 1977.

United 6125 (HHN 725D), London, 1977

On loan to National Travel and seen working duplicate on the long 201 service from Sedgefield, 6125 was a Bristol RE with an ECW coach body, fitted with two-part folding doors. With eighty-four vehicles, United was the biggest operator of this type. United numbered its vehicles by type: the 12xx series as express coaches; the 61xx series for downgraded local coaches; and the 43xx series, indicating local buses, often in NBC red bus livery, which was unique to United on this type. 6125 was only ever used by United. Being withdrawn in 1978 after being stored for two years, it was sold for scrap to Booths in December 1978. (Alan Snatt)

United 1151 (OPT 852D)

United was in some way similar to Crosville; both had solid Bristol/ECW fleets until a number of non-standards added variety. In United's case it was the acquisition of Wilkinson, Gillett, Shaw Brothers and some transferred East Yorkshire vehicles that introduced some fascinating vehicles to the fleet. 1151 had come from Gillett Brothers, Quarrington Hill, with the 1974 takeover. United had five Plaxton Highwaymans, but only 1151 was in dual-purpose configuration, which also made it unique in the NBC. (Omnibus Society)

United 1153 (KUP 201J)

Also a former Gillett Brother vehicle, 1153 was one of a four with the more commonplace Plaxton Derwent bodywork, of which a pair (1152/3) were painted in local coach livery. Only West Riding, South Wales and later Ribble (ex-West Riding) had similar-liveried vehicles in the NBC. KUP 201J found further use with Rhodes Coaches (West Yorkshire) and Eagre of Gainsborough. (Omnibus Society)

United 1171 (TUP 269M)

Another former Gillett Brothers vehicle was 1171, a 1974 Bedford YRT with Duple C53F bodywork. Nearly new when taken over by United, they soon disposed of it in 1978. Still relatively new, it found further use independents in North East Wales and Devon. (Omnibus Society)

United 1000 (160 FYV)

Certainly a contender for the National Bus Company's most unusual local coach, United's 1000 was a Bedford J2SZ10 with Plaxton C16F bodywork, and was new to Timpson, Catford, in 1963. United purchased it in 1975, specifically for the transfer service to Teesside Airport near Durham. It operated briefly still in Timpson's livery, before United painted it and lettered it above the windows 'TEESSIDE AIRPORT'. After withdrawal it saw a few years with independents in Scotland and West Yorkshire. (Omnibus Society)

United 4297 (FHN 851J), Pickering Garage, July 1982

United operated large numbers of Bristol REs in all configurations. 4267, recently having been renumbered from 6051, was a RELH6G with bus-bodied ECW DP49F bodywork new in May 1971. Seen outside Pickering Garage, behind is glimpsed 6151 (NHN 787K (formerly 1287)), another Bristol RELH6G but with Plaxton bodywork, downgraded to dual-purpose livery. 6051 would be withdrawn in 1984.

National Bus Company Dual Purpose Vehicles

United 6212 (LGR 412T), Wembley Stadium

New in 1978, 6212 was a Leyland Leopard/Plaxton Supreme new to United in local coach livery. Later the degree of white would be increased, as on 6212 below. This batch would find use with Northumbria and Tees & District after privatisation. (Alan Snatt)

United 6201 (ABR 865S), Melrose, 1985

Working the 508 Edinburgh to Newcastle via Jedburgh, 6201 is seen in the border market town of Melrose. In the mid-1980s, the rules on livery application relaxed, and subsequently United increased the amount of white on a number of their grant coaches. 6201 was a Leyland Leopard/Duple Dominant – very much a standard NBC local coach of the mid-1980s.

United Counties 129 (32 DRB), Bedford Bus Station

The Nottingham registration gives a clue to this vehicle's past. Bristol MW 32 DRB had an interesting history; new to Midland General in 1958, it would be transferred to Mansfield District in 1971 and then to United Counties in June 1973. It would serve with UCOC until August 1976, when it was sold for scrap to Martins of Middlewich. United Counties operated six second-hand MWs, all with a similar history. At least two carried this livery, and most would finish their service retaining coach seats but in NBC bus green. (Transport Library)

United Counties 252 (ABD 252B), Basingstoke Bus Station

Operating a Royal Blue service to Bournemouth, 252 is seen at Basingstoke bus station around 1974. This vehicle, like several similar Bristol RE coaches in the United Counties fleet, would be painted into local coach colours, before being painted at a later date into National coach white. Withdrawn in November 1980, it survives in preservation. Note Hants & Dorset Bristol L5G towing vehicle 9082 in the background. (Transport Library)

National Bus Company Dual Purpose Vehicles 75

United Counties 297 (92 FXD), Bedford Bus Station, 2 March 1974

Another takeover by United Counties that introduced interesting vehicles was Birch Brothers in 1969. Twelve Leyland Leopards were acquired with a mix of Willowbrook (two), Park Royal (six) and Marshall (four) bodywork. All were classed as dual-purpose, but only one, Park Royal 192 (92 FXD), received NBC local coach livery. The Park Royal batch, 190–5 (90–95 FXD), had issues with water leaking in around the front. After attempting some in-house repairs, the company sent 192 to Southfield Coachworks of Loughborough in November 1973 for rectification work, where it was fitted with a Seddon-style front end. Renumbered 239 in February 1974, it was withdrawn in the following November. It found further use in North Staffordshire with Berresfords (Cheddleton), an operator of numerous ex-NBC vehicles. (Michael Penn)

United Counties 201 (YXD 459M), 200 (LXD 536K) and 202 (YXD 458M), Luton Garage

Court Line was an early example of a budget airline, but it also operated a number of stage service in the Luton, Dunstable and Hemel Hempstead areas. When it collapsed in 1974, United Counties stepped in to cover some of these routes, and with them came eight non-standard Ford R192 and R1014 coaches fitted with forty-five-seat Plaxton Elite (Express II/Express III) bodies. The eight vehicles were allocated to Luton Garage. Some operated briefly in Court Line two-tone green livery with United Counties NBC fleet names. *Buses Annual* of 1977 contained an informative article on United Counties' second-hand vehicles of this era. (Alan Snatt)

National Bus Company Dual Purpose Vehicles

United Counties 207 (YNV 207J), Derby Bus Station

Even with its coach-type seating, this Bristol RE perhaps isn't the most suitable vehicle to hire to National Travel East. United Counties had classed some of these vehicles as coaches in National coach white, so perhaps they thought differently. United Counties had dual-purpose Bristol RE/ECWs with both flat and the restyled curved fronts, as seen on 207 at Derby in the mid-1970s as it works service 557, which had originated in either Mansfield or possibly even further north. The application of this livery to bus-bodied Bristol RE/ECWs varied between NBC fleets; United Counties painted the white down to the lower trim moulding, which avoided a step after the windscreen.

West Riding 266 (GHD 413G), Wakefield Bus Station, August 1973

The Alexander Y-type was a regular sight on the roads of Yorkshire, with East Yorkshire, West Riding, Yorkshire Traction and SYPTE all having examples. 266 was part of a batch of five dating from 1969 that had been used by both Yorkshire Woollen and Hebble previously. Note the single fleet name; it would later carry the joint West Riding/Yorkshire Woollen fleet names in small letters above each other. West Riding would eventually downgrade this vehicle to a bus and paint it poppy red with a thin white centre band. (Grahame Wareham)

West Riding 381 (HWY 721N), Wakefield Bus Station

West Riding 381 was a Leyland Leopard PSU3B/4R with the restyled front Alexander Y-type DP49F bodywork. The fleets of West Riding and Yorkshire Woollen were amalgamated in the mid-1970s, after which coaches and service vehicles usually carried the non-standard-size fleet names of both companies. 381 is seen earlier than the joining and therefore only carries West Riding fleet name with an early red double-N symbol. West Riding often displayed the fleet name on the front and rear of the vehicles. Additionally, it usually picked out the grille mouldings on some Alexander-bodied vehicles in white.

West Riding/Yorkshire Woollen 4 (PWW 709R), Selby Bus Station, 21 May 1977

Displaying the joint fleet name in use in the late 1970s and early 1980s, West Riding/Yorkshire Woollen 4 is a Leyland Leopard with an Alexander T-type DP49F body. This body type was never as common in the NBC as its predecessor, the Alexander Y-type.

Yorkshire Woollen 130 (9731 AT)

Images of Yorkshire Woollen vehicles in NBC local coach livery are rare, mainly because of the very small number of vehicles that could have carried the livery with the single 'Yorkshire' fleet name. 130, a Leyland Leopard with a Willowbrook DP47F body, was formerly East Yorkshire 731 until 1976. Yorkshire Woollen only had four other vehicles classed as dual-purpose, all ex-Hebble, BET-bodied AEC Reliances, and at least one, 275 (KCP 808G), received local coach livery. Once the fleet was fully joined with West Riding, both names would appear together, in a smaller font, on local coach-painted vehicles.

West Yorkshire 1091 (7904 WY), Harrogate Bus Station

West Yorkshire Bristol MW 1091, a Bristol MW/ECW DP41F, was a bus-style body but fitted with coach seats. The non-standard application of the fleet name may have been either due to the availability of red transfers, or the fact West Yorkshire had a number of MWs with coach-style bodies with roof lights, necessitating the positioning of the fleet name on the side. Perhaps the company wanted them to appear the same?

West Yorkshire 2524 (CWY 503H), Blackpool Coliseum Coach Station

Unlike 2515 seen below, 2524 was built with a single coach door and small destination blinds. A Bristol RELH6L, CWY 503H was new in May 1970 as CRL6, being renumbered 1035 in 1971. When West Yorkshire grouped dual-purpose vehicles into the 23xx/25xx series in 1978, it became 2305 and finally 2524 in 1979. Withdrawn in 1981, it passed to the NBC disposal centre at Bracebridge Heath near Lincoln, where it was broken up.

West Yorkshire 2515 (YWY 514G), PMT Newcastle Garage

In 1977/78, West Yorkshire sent seven of its Bristol RELH6G/ECW DP47F vehicles for refurbishment by Willowbrook. The result, which externally involved rebuilding the entire front, was radically different in appearance. Numbered 2501/2513–8, all were finished in local coach livery. The first conversion, AWR 401B (2501), was initially rebuilt with a larger, deeper front window, but was later rebuilt to match the rest. 2515 (formerly 1026) is seen at PMT Newcastle Garage. It was withdrawn from Leeds in early 1981, and, like all the others, was scrapped in 1982.

West Yorkshire 2562 (OWY 664T), London, Hyde Park Corner

After the company's experiment in rebuilding Bristol REs by Willowbrook, they purchased more conventional grant-specification vehicles. New in 1978, 2562 was a Leyland Leopard with a Plaxton DP49F body. Part of a batch of thirty-two, the first three had Duple bodies.

West Yorkshire 2578 (KUB 552V), Blackpool Coliseum Coach Station

In the late 1970s West Yorkshire purchased a number of grant-specification coaches, which were delivered in local coach livery from new. All Leyland Leopards with Duple or Plaxton bodies, 2578 had the revised Plaxton Supreme body.

National Bus Company Dual Purpose Vehicles

Western National 1231 (281 KTA), Bideford Pill Bus Stand

As part of the NBC, the Western National/Devon General company had a huge operating area; even after transferring its Wiltshire operations to Bristol, it still covered Cornwall, Devon and large parts of Somerset and Dorset. One of the more unusual types it operated was the Bristol SUS/SUL. Western National (with Southern National) was by far the largest user of this type, having 133. Unique for an NBC constituent were the thirty-six dual-purpose versions, which had two front designs. The more finished style is seen on 1231, parked at Bideford *c*. 1978. Interestingly, only one, 1220 (270 KTA), was painted in red/white local coach colours for Devon General.

Western National 2905 (XUO 724), Exeter Coach Station

New as 2241 in 1958 for the 'Royal Blue' fleet, 2905 had been repainted in green and white in September 1973. Allocated to Barnstable, it would be withdrawn in 1980. Western National also operated bus-bodied Bristol MWs (without roof lights) in this livery.

National Bus Company Dual Purpose Vehicles

Western National 1237 (890 ADV), St Austell Garage, 1977

One of the most unusual vehicles to receive NBC local coach livery was 1237, a sole example in the NBC of a 1959 AEC Reliance with a Willowbrook Viking C41F body. Working with Greenslades until 1970, Western National retained this single example for tour work in the St Austell area. Withdrawn in the later 1970s, it survives preserved in Devon General (Grey Cars) livery. Maybe one day it will return to leaf green/white? (Transport Library)

Western National 1472 (RDV 423H), Bideford Pill Bus Stand

Like many other NBC constituents, Western National downgraded the ECW coach-bodied Bristol RELH to dual-purpose work. A 'Royal Blue' NBC white coach up to 1979, 1472 was one of six converted to DP45F, though retaining a single leaf door. Interestingly, Western National never operated the bus-bodied Bristol RE in local coach livery. 1472 survives in preservation.

Devon General 1469 (RDV 420H), Paignton Garage

In the same batch as 1472 above, 1469 was the only example to receive Devon General red/white local coach livery. It received this livery in 1978, retaining it until 1981, when Western National repainted it in green/white with 'Cornish Fairways' lettering. 1469 is also preserved.

Devon General 2501 (PUO 501M)

A batch of seven vehicles new in 1974/5 were, unusually for this style of coach body, delivered in local coach livery from new. Some of this batch were repainted into NBC green local coach livery, with Devon General fleet names, while others received broad red band livery. 2501 was withdrawn by Devon General in 1983; at the same time, some of the batch passed to the North Devon subsidiary fleet.

Western National 3304 (AFJ 724T), Laira Workshops, Plymouth

3304 was part of a batch of fourteen Bristol LH6Ls with Plaxton C43F bodies, divided between Royal Blue and Western National. New in 1979, and delivered in local coach livery, 3304 would serve with Western National until 1995, when it was sold to a local independent operator.

Western National 1332 (JFJ 497N), St Austell Bus Station, 1984

1332 was one of twelve Elite IIIs to be built in 1975 on Bristol LH6L chassis for Greenslades. They were only 7 feet 6 inches and were especially suited to rural roads of Cornwall and Somerset. Transfered in 1978, it initially continued in National white with Devon General fleet names, being repainted in green/white in April 1979 for Western National. Seen here lettered 'Cornwall Busways', it survived into the privatised Western National fleet.

Southern National 3100 (PTT 70R), Bridgwater Bus Station, 3 May 1983

The Western National batch of Bristol LH6L with Plaxton C43F bodies lasted long enough for examples to enter all the subsidiary fleets formed before privatisation. 3100 carries Southern National fleet names when seen at Bridgwater in 1983.

Western National 3315 (AFJ 735T), Barnstable Bus Station

Fitted with the narrow body, Bristol LH6L 3315 was transferred to Devon General in 1983 and then passed into the North Devon (Red Bus) fleet, which was formed as a precursor to privatisation.

National Bus Company Dual Purpose Vehicles

Devon General 3509 (VOD 626S), Exeter Bus Station

3509 started life in 1978 as a National white coach in the Royal Blue fleet of Western National. Downgraded into the Devon General fleet, it also carried Greenslades NBC venetian blind livery. It was later sold for further use in East Yorkshire.

Western Welsh UD4966 (HBO 383D), Cardiff Bus Station, 3 April 1976

Western Welsh and Rhondda operated a number of dual-purpose Leyland Leopard BET-bodied vehicles. Though initially similar, UD4966 was a Leyland Tiger Cub with shorter Marshall DP41F bodywork. When in the National Welsh fleet, it would be downgraded to bus status in poppy red, but retained its coach seats and extra trim.

National Bus Company Dual Purpose Vehicles 87

Western Welsh UD768 (PTX 830F), Cardiff Bus Station, *c.* **1974**

UD768, an AEC Reliance 6MU4R/Plaxton C41F, was new in February 1968 to Neath & Cardiff Luxury Coaches. Transferred to Western Welsh in 1971, it was renumbered UD4368 in the mid-1970s. It survives today preserved in N&C brown livery, fittingly in South Wales.

Jones (Western Welsh) UC1463J (TCK 715), Aberbeeg Bus Garage

Leyland Leopard/Harrington Cavalier TCK 715 was new in 1963 with Ribble. Acquired in 1973, it received this mixed livery with pre-NBC Jones fleet names and the National Bus Company logo. One of four, they passed to Red & White in 1974/5. Jones had also bought its own Harrington-bodied coaches from new. (Alan Snatt)

Jones (Western Welsh) RD173 (HAX 305L), Aberbeeg Bus Garage

Unusually retaining the pre-NBC fleet name style on the corporate livery, Jones RD173 stands in the Warn Turn Garage yard at Aberbeeg. RD173 was one of three similar vehicles that Jones owned. (Alan Snatt)

Jones (Western Welsh) RD174 (OWO 309M), Aberbeeg Bus Garage, 21 September 1974

Jones of Aberbeeg was allowed to retain its blue livery into the NBC corporate era. A small fleet operating out of one garage in Aberbeeg, it was managed by Western Welsh. Seen here is RD174, a 1972 Bristol RELH6L with an Eastern Coachworks DP49F body in rare NBC blue and white local coach livery. The company's numbering formed a vehicle code. Thus, RD174 could be interpreted as follows: RD (**R**ear engine, **D**ual-purpose), 174 (new in 1974).

Jones (Western Welsh) UC1974 (OWO 311M), Aberbeeg Bus Garage, 21 September 1974

Jones had two Leyland Leopard PSU3/Duple Dominant Express C53F. Though numbered UC (Underfloor engine, Coach), both were initially painted in local coach livery. Similar UC1973 was later repainted into National white while still in the Jones fleet. When Jones was absorbed into National Welsh, this vehicle became UD1135 in red/white local coach livery.

Rhondda (Western Welsh) UD4565 (DBO 150C), Cardiff Bus Station

Like Jones, Rhondda had a small number of vehicles in local coach livery. UD4565 had carried Western Welsh fleet names in this livery but later received Rhondda ones. It was part of a batch of six Plaxton Panorama C36F-bodied AEC 2MU4RA Reliances placed into service in 1965, numbered 150–5. Re-seated to C38F in 1965/6 and then to C40F in 1966/7, it was renumbered from 150 to UD165 in August 1974 and then to UD4565 in October 1975. Withdrawn in 1977, it passed to independent operator Weaver of Tredegar in September 1978. It was to finish up much further from home, however, moving to A. P. Enterprises of Sri Lanka in November 1979. Operating from Porth Garage, Western Welsh retained the Rhondda fleet name until it was combined into National Welsh in 1978. The only other type Rhondda operated in local coach livery were Leyland Tiger Cubs with Willowbrook BET bodies. Rhondda had used an attractive green/white livery for dual-purpose vehicles before the NBC corporate image.

Red & White DS759 (UWO 707), Newport Bus Station

New in 1959, DS759 was delivered as a coach. After a period on loan to South Wales it was repainted as seen here and renumbered UD759, and later UD5759. Withdrawal came in May 1976. (Alan Snatt)

Red & White UC263 (24 FAX), Cheltenham Coach Station, *c.* 1974

UC263, a Bristol MW6G/ECW C39F, was new in 1963. As built this vehicle had roof quarter lights, which were panelled over in 1972. Western Welsh constituents did not always change the code on downgraded coaches, though in local coach livery it still carries the UC code, which should have been changed to UD. Briefly renumbered UC5863, in was sold in late 1975.

Red & White UC463 (26 FAX), Cardiff Bus Station, *c.* 1974

In the same batch as UC263 above, UD463 has had the same modification to the roof quarter lights. Allocated to Cardiff, it was renumbered to UC5863 in October 1975, and it was withdrawn soon afterwards.

Red & White ND5275 (KDW 360P), Cardiff Bus Station, 1976

A total of thirty-five dual-purpose Leyland Nationals were delivered to Western Welsh (eighteen), Red & White (sixteen) and Jones (two). All took delivery of the 11.3-metre-long DP48F version. New in November 1975, and intended for Western Welsh, but allocated to Red & White, ND5275 is seen here on the long service 73 to Gloucester – the sort of duty these vehicles were intended for. After serving with National Welsh as ND1414, it returned to the reformed Red & White fleet, and was route branded for this same service.

National Welsh RD4669 (SAX 2G), Bulwark Workshops, Chepstow

New to Red & White as RC269, RD4669 had operated in National white with red National Welsh fleet names before being repainted in red/white local coach livery in November 1979. It would remain in use until 1983.

National Welsh RD1368 (CWO 289K) and UD1288 (TKG 508J), Chepstow Garage, July 1983

Two classic NWOC dual-purpose types reflect the origins of the company, Bristol RE/ECW RD1368 coming from Red & White and Leyland Leopard PSU4/Willowbrook UD1288 from Western Welsh. By the time they were seen here, both had been renumbered, formerly being RD4072 and UD2871 respectively.

National Bus Company Dual Purpose Vehicles

National Welsh MD1377 (SKG 892S)

At a time when an NBC minibus was a rarity, Western Welsh obtained two batches of Asco-bodied Leyland 440EAs. The three delivered in 1977 were seated DP20F, and in 1978 four were re-seated to DP19F. National Welsh was not the only NBC subsidiary to buy these: Bristol had one from 1973, and Alder Valley bought three in 1974. MD1377 became NWOC service vehicle E25 in December 1981, finally being withdrawn by the company in March 1983. Though fitted with coach seating, National Welsh painted a few in unrelieved poppy red bus livery.

National Welsh UD270 (SKG 179H), Swansea Quadrant Bus Station

National Welsh downgraded numerous coaches into dual-purpose roles in the mid-1980s. UD270 was a Leyland Leopard/Plaxton C49F. Originally with National white coach livery when operating with Jones of Abergeeg, the coach door was retained. Although not ideal for stage work, it at least retains its chrome-finish mouldings, as NWOC occasionally painted over these with red.

National Welsh UD576 (NWO 450R)

A typical NBC vehicle of the era, and delivered in National white, Leyland Leopard/Duple Dominant I UD576 was in local coach livery when caught parked by an unidentified National Welsh garage. It finished its time with OK Travel in the North East.

National Welsh UD1134 (OWO 310M), Cardiff Bus Station

Originally UC1874, this vehicle started life with Jones as one of a pair (the other, UC1974, was illustrated in the Jones section above). Looking somewhat different with a modified grille, UD1134 stands in Cardiff bus station. Note the Green Line coach in the background.

National Bus Company Dual Purpose Vehicles 95

National Welsh UD1181 (KWO 562X), Swansea Quadrant Bus Station

In the mid-1980s National Welsh developed an extensive network of limited-stop services, with route branded grant-specification coaches in a variation of the NBC venetian blind livery. Though a good marketing move when used on the correct route, if vehicles were used for other duties it could cause confusion. In such a case, UD1181, a Leyland Leopard/Willowbrook C46F, is seen off route at Swansea. This vehicle also carried fleet numbers UC8108 and UC181.

Yorkshire Traction 14 (FHE 333D), Huddersfield Bus Station

Yorkshire Traction 14 was a Leyland Leopard/Plaxton Panorama C47F. From a batch of ten dating from 1965/6, this was the only one to be repainted into local coach livery, the rest retaining National white. Withdrawal came around 1979, after which it was preserved in the North West in for a couple of years.

Yorkshire Traction 216 (JHE 516E), Blackpool Coliseum Coach Station

Before the arrival of grant-specification coaches, the Yorkshire Traction dual-purpose fleet was made up of Alexander Y- and T-types and Marshall BET-style vehicles. With the later bodywork, 216 was a Leyland Leopard of 1968 vintage. With large panoramic windows and dual headlights, these were impressive-looking vehicles. 216 is seen at the Blackpool Coliseum coach station in the 1970s – a location where interesting vehicles from numerous NBC fleets could be found alongside each other. (Alan Snatt)

Yorkshire Traction 252 (PWB 252R), Crosville Sealand Road Workshops

Working an excursion, Yorkshire Traction 252 is seen at the unlikely location of Crosville's Central Workshops in Chester. This may have been the destination of the visit, as an NBC vehicle in need of assistance would have probably gone to the company's Liverpool Road garage. 252 was from an order for two Leyland Leopard/Duple C49Fs – the first grant coaches bought by YTC. Both would later be painted in National white.